Delight!

READ Model to Design Remarkable Services

Anshuman Sharma

Dedication

To my Family

CONTENTS

Introduction

This work is the sister book of the previously published material on product design. Both of these books use the similar methodology only the context has been changed to services in this book.

Service design is an activity of planning and organizing resources, people, infrastructure, communication and other components to improve the interaction between the service provider and consumer. The aim is to satisfy the customer, who receives the service, with the quality of the service delivery and its value addition in the life of the customer. The objective of the service design methodologies is to understand the needs of the customers and considering the constraints of the service provider design the service which is user friendly, efficient, effective and suiting the needs of the customers. These design methodologies requires experts from the various domains to work in multifunctional teams for designing successful services. Service design is an activity that suggests behavioral patterns or 'scripts' to the players interacting in the service, which gives overall flexibility in the service delivery. A successful service needs to be unique and should be according to the requirements of the customers. A good service becomes its own marketer as every time it is used, it delights its users, which makes them the advocates of the service. We can observe this phenomenon in some of the winning services in the market.

Few companies have mastered the art of service design and they are extremely successful in the market with high profitability and growth. These companies use the service design skills as their competitive advantage and protect it like trade secret. In fact, the process of creating great services is not complex. It is a set of tools and methods which, if used properly and sincerely, can support any design team to develop amazing services. We have tried to expose these methods and devices in this work.

To contrast the available books on service design methods, we have kept this book extremely simple. The specified devices can be used by any person looking to design services. The simplicity of the devices is evident from the fact that even a layperson, with no knowledge about service design, can understand and use these devices. The services are differentiated by their value proposition, quality of delivery and features. A great design of service evolves mainly from the attitude and culture of the organization rather than any technical expertise.

It has always been difficult for companies to create great services. Some companies hire highly qualified technical experts to create the magic, while others outsource the service design process. Sometimes the responsibilities of creating new ideas and services lie on few elite individuals, who use random methods & techniques to think and analyze the design of the services. In most cases these efforts fail. The main reason for this failure is the wrong approach.

The most important aspect for developing new ideas about services and subsequently designing it requires a proper methodology, which is generally simple but effective. Every successful company has their set of methods to design the services but the fundamental ideas remain same. This book tries to reveal the effective but simple methodology of designing the great services.

The methodology discussed in the book has four segments and is called READ Technique. READ stands for **R**esearch, **E**xperience, **A**nalyze and **D**iscover. 'Research segment' focuses on capturing and analyzing the information available in the market, 'Experience segment' focuses on checking out the views and ideas generated, 'Analyze Segment' focuses on observing the aspects for service and 'Discover Segment' focuses on surveys and interviews. Each of the four segments has several devices and methods specified in this work which would help the professionals in designing great and winning services.

To design a great service the designers need to focus on a specific area of the design process. The specified segments and devices in the book would serve the designers by focusing their attention to each area of the design process. Each device described in the book briefly describes it, specifies its importance & value, explain the way to use it and supported by an example to describe it.

The design devices list specified in this book is exhaustive and every device would not be suitable for your projects. Design team needs to identify and list the devices to be used for a specific project. These devices would motivate the design team in various ways by suggesting them relevant methods to solve the design problem.

It is suggested that this resource should be used as a guide and reference to create better service designs.

RESEARCH SEGMENT

Research segment of the READ Model includes the devices which focus on collecting and researching the available data, information, insights in archives, published or tacit format. This segment equips the designers with substantial grasp of the project to graduate to other segments of the model.

Device 1: Research - Scenario Analysis

Check with various scenarios to identify different ways which would create operational difficulties for the service.

This device would help the designer to identify the various situations when the service would not be delivered properly to the consumer.

Identify various scenarios which can create operational difficulties for the service. Find the reasons for these problems. These can be through human mistakes, negligence or actions. The purpose is to design flexible services which would function properly even during problems.

Example: Identify various ways which could affect the courier delivery to design flexible service processes.

Device 2: Research - Salability

Check for the salability of the planned service.

This analysis is important as the designed service should be marketable and commercially viable.

Conduct a market survey asking the target segment about their intention to consume the service based upon features, value proposition and pricing.

Example: Designers checked the salability of the newly designed online service based upon its features, value proposition, interactivity, user friendliness and pricing.

Device 3: Research - Extreme Conditions

Check the ability of the potential service providers to deliver the service in extreme conditions.

This test is important to establish the quality and robustness of the service design while it is delivered and consumed in extreme conditions.

Identify the extreme conditions and test the service design in these extreme conditions which may include weather, crisis, emergencies and disasters.

Example: Designers checked the robustness of medical service delivery in extreme conditions.

Device 4: Research - Legality

The design of the service should be in accordance to government's rules, laws and regulations.

The knowledge of these factors is important as slight neglect of any regulation, law or rule, while designing the service and its processes, can have acute impact on the business and service delivery.

The analysis of each and every rule, policy, regulation and law related to the service and its design needs is important before finalizing the service design, as all related factors to design must lie within the government legal framework. The design should also be flexible enough to integrate any future changes in the rules, regulations and laws.

Example: Before finalizing the design of healthcare services it needs to be checked for its conformance to all Government rules, laws and regulations.

Device 5: Research - Assumptions

Identify all assumptions while designing the service and check them for their practicality.

Designers need to know about all of our assumptions and their sensitivities to estimate the effectiveness of the service design.

Check for all the assumptions we have taken for designing the service. Designers need to check the sensitivity of each assumption. The objective should be to design a sustainable service for the market.

<u>Example</u>: Designers identified all assumptions while designing the new financial product and service and checked it for their practicality and generality.

Device 6: Research - Efficiency Analysis

This device focuses on the efficiency of the service delivery.

The inefficiencies and blockages in the service processes would become evident with this device.

Identify all the activities and processes of the system and check them for their efficiencies and flow. Check for the inadequacies and problems of the system for taking corrective actions.

Example: Designing effective navigation of a website.

Device 7: Research - Past trends Analysis

This device analyzes the past trends which have affected the design of the service.

This device would clarify the relation of market trends with the service design and would help the designers in future designs of the service.

List all the past trends of the market and the corresponding design of the service. Analyze the major factors which affected the design of the service over the course of evolution of the service and its delivery. Understand the clear relation of the service design with the market trends. Use this relation to design services.

Example: The relation of market trends affecting the design of the data services.

Device 8: Research - Design Publications

Get ideas and insights from the worldwide design publications.

Design publications report the latest trends, ideas and developments in the service design domain. The views, information and insights from these publications would help the designers to use the latest devices, tools and methods to design winning services.

Subscribe to the best design publications and research content available in the market, which would keep the designers up-to-date with the latest ideas, technologies and insights. Designers can use this knowledge to design better services at lower cost.

Device 9: Research - Trends and Design

Establish the relation between market trends and service design.

This device helps in integrating the market trends in the design and delivery of service.

Differentiate between long term and short term market trends which affect the service design and delivery. It is important to notice that even short term trends impacts the design of the service. Study the past trends of the market and analyze their effect on the design of the service. Create a specific relationship between trends and service design. Analyze the present market trends and modify the service design based on these powerful trends. Designers should equip themselves with an effective system to analyze the long term trends of the market and their impact on the design of the services.

Example: The entertainment events design changes with the trends.

Device 10: Research - Visualize Future

Use forecasting methods to predict the changes in the market.

This understanding would help in creating sustainable designs of the services.

Use established forecasting methods to forecast the evolution of the service. Also, predict the future market trends. This understanding would help in integrating these factors to create a robust design of the service.

<u>Example</u>: Forecasting in news services would help in better design of news delivery.

Device 11: Research - One-time Consumers

Analyze one-time consumers of similar services to know their behaviors and attitudes.

This analysis would clarify the weaknesses of the existing services which are responsible for not able to attract repeat consumers. This learning can be used to create services which would have high percentage of repeat consumers.

Identify the unsuccessful similar services in the market which are not able to attract repeat consumers. Explore the characteristics and design elements of these services which are responsible for their failure. Use this learning to design better services.

Example: Analysis of the failed restaurants in a metropolitan city gave enough learning to the designers to design a fast-food center.

Device 12: Research - Service Evolution

Check for the evolution of the services (related to the project) to design future services.

This analysis helps in understanding the design changes in the service and guides the designers with insights of the service evolution while explaining the reasons for the design changes in past.

Look at the history of the service and study the various designs elements and operational processes of the past. Identify the reasons which are responsible for forcing the changes in service design. This evolution can be extrapolated to get design ideas about the service.

Example: Looking at the evolution of the design of news services would help the designer to plan for business news services.

Device 13: Research - Present Trends Analysis

It analyzes the current trends of the market, which would affect the value requirement of the service.

This device would indicate the new design requirements of the service.

Identify all the current trends of the market and industry which would affect the demand of the market. Analyze these trends to understand their impact on the consumption and design of the service.

<u>Example</u>: Fashion trends affecting the dressing of the students.

Device 14: Research - Future View

Analyze the future changes in the market and the service demands of the consumers.

The device is useful in keeping the designers ahead of the market demand by preparing them for drastic changes in the demands of the consumers.

Use the statistical tools and forecasting methods to predict, with high confidence levels, the future of the industry and needs of target customer segments. Utilize this analysis and forecast to develop the service design plans and to allocate resources.

Example: Use forecasting methods to understand the required changes in financial service industry to introduce new services.

Device 15: Research - Micro Analysis

This device analyzes the micro aspects of the processes and system involved in using the service.

Micro Analysis is used to extract the hidden aspects related to service, which can affect the final design of the service.

Identify all the processes associated with the service and analyze the details of each process. Check for hidden issues and concerns which would affect the design of service. Identify the required modifications in the service design.

Example: Several hidden aspects were revealed with Micro-Analysis while designing the play-school for kids.

Device 16: Research - Other Industries Designers

Capture the insights of the designers from other industries.

This device helps the designers by equipping them with the suggestions and ideas of other design professionals who bring in fresh perspectives.

Identify the best designers of other industries and meet them to take their suggestions and views about the design of your services. These people would bring in new ideas and perspectives which could help the designers in creating a better service.

Example: The design of a department store was improved with the suggestions of other designers.

Device 17: Research - Relationships study

Use this device to find the relationship between various elements of the service, its processes and their environments.

This device is useful in looking for opportunities in the relationships existing in the environment of the service. These insights would give us new ideas about improving the design of the service.

Understand the environment of the service in detail and identify the various relationships in it. Draw the relationship diagram between these elements. Look for the missing aspects and potential issues to generate new design ideas. Integrate the identified facts in the design of the service.

Example: To design a new bus stand, look for the various environments in which it would be used by commuters to check hidden issues and innovation opportunities.

Device 18: Research - Physical Attributes Analysis

For a new market check for the physical aspects feasibility of the target users of the service.

This device helps in modifying or creating the services to suit the physical aspects of the target population.

Use secondary data to analyze the physical attributes of the target population which would include physical aspects like height, weight, size of limbs etc. The service should be designed keeping these aspects in mind and tested thoroughly in the target market. It is important to note that for any new market this analysis and test has to be conducted to launch suitable services in the market.

Example: The design of the seating arrangement of multiplex was modified with physical attributes analysis.

Device 19: Research - Demographic Study

Study the demographic factors of the targeted population.

This study is important to establish the impact of demographics factors like gender, age, income, and education etc. of the target customers on the service design.

Check demographic data from private and public sources to analyze the required aspects of the targeted area. Check for the impact of these factors on the design on the services currently being used by them. Integrate these factors in the design of the new service.

Example: The design of physical care services would differ based upon demographic factors.

Device 20: Research - Psychographic Study

Study the Psychographic factors of the targeted population.

This study is important to establish the impact of psychographic like social classes, interests, activities, attitudes and lifestyle etc. of the target customers on the service design.

Check psychographic data from private and public sources to analyze the relevant factors of the targeted area. Check for the impact of these factors on the design on the services being used by them. Integrate these factors in the design of the service.

<u>Example</u>: The design of social clubs would differ based upon psychographic factors.

Device 21: Research - Repeat Consumers

Analyze repeat consumers to know their behaviors and attitudes.

This analysis would clarify the strength of the existing services which have dedicated repeat consumers. This learning can be used to create services which would have high percentage of repeat consumers.

Identify the successful service providers in the market with high percentage of repeat consumers. Explore the features, characteristics and design elements of these popular services which make them attractive and exclusive. Use this learning to design sticky services.

Example: Analysis of customer's experience at reputed bank branches gave enough learning to develop and design a successful telecom network providers 'customer contact centers'.

Device 22: Research - Secondary Research

Collect and analyze all the published data and information about target market.

Secondary research gives the designers the various perspectives and extensive historical data to analyze the market.

Check for all the appropriate published data by private and public sources to analyze the various aspects of the targeted population.

Example: The design of houses at a location requires extensive secondary research to understand the various factors which are required to be considered.

Device 23: Research - Behavioral Study

Segmenting the potential customers based upon their behaviors and personalities.

It is important as segmenting would clarify the communication methodology to various segments of the customer group. Each customer segment would act as a niche and the value proposition of the service and its design aspects can be communicated in the effective way to each type of customers, for maximum impact.

Analyze your target population and identify various personality and behavioral parameters grouping the customers. Segment them based upon their personalities, behaviors and lifestyles. Identify the impactful communication strategy for each segment.

Example: A restaurant can offer various meal packs and services for different customer segments.

Device 24: Research - Competitive Analysis

Analyze the competitors of the service and company in the market.

This device is helpful in creating benchmarks for service and its design. This analysis also clarifies the main ideas and competencies of competitors about the service delivery and improvement.

Collect all required data and information about the competitors and competing services in the market. Analyze this data for creating performance standards, benchmarks and value propositions.

Example: To design a new data service, analyzing the present players, their strengths & weaknesses, market offerings, features, value propositions and designs of all top services is necessary.

Device 25: Research - Cultural Differences

Analyze the differences in cultures at various places.

This device is helpful in understanding and appreciating the differences in cultures and designing or modifying the service accordingly.

Use available information & data to analyze and understand the culture of the targeted area and population for which the service is to be designed. It is also important to check cultural differences of other locations, where the service could be used in future. The service design decision should be taken based upon these differences.

Example: The design of the modular kitchens may differ in various cultures and places.

Device 26: Research - Other Markets

Study other markets for similar services and customers to get new learning, knowledge and ideas.

This understanding would help the designers to get the ideas about the existing service designs in use and their limitations, weaknesses and strengths. They can use this information to design a more suitable and better service.

Identify all the markets with similar needs and requirements and the services currently available in these markets. Analyze these services in detail for all required aspects. Incorporate these insights in the new design of the services.

Example: To design a public utility service at a crowded place, designers evaluated the similar services available in other metropolitan cities.

Device 27: Research - Third Person Analysis

The designer analyzes the service and its design as a third person, not connected to the project in any way.

This is useful in getting an unbiased and fresh view about the service.

Third person is an independent person and in no way related to any of the stakeholders of the project and company. Ask your designers to consider themselves as a third person for their service and analyze it critically as an outsider.

Example: To improve the service design the designers formed a multidimensional team to analyze their design for playschools in the market.

Device 28: Research - Customer Delight

Check for the various features, characteristics and design aspect of the service which would delight the consumers.

This device helps in understanding the thinking process of end-users better by understanding their emotional connection with the service.

Collect the information and insights available in the market about the various features and design aspects of the services which are appreciated by the customers. These ideas can be analyzed for their integration in the service design.

Example:

To design the food court in the multiplex the designers analyzed the existing food-courts available in the various malls in different cities for design aspects and to answer the question "Why is it successful?"

Device 29: Research - Customer Dislikes

Check for the various features and design aspects of the related services, which are unpopular in the market.

This analysis would help the designers by warning them for the features and design aspects, which would be disliked by the end-users.

Collect the information and insights available in the market about the various features and design aspects of the services which are unpopular. These insights can be analyzed to understand the thinking process of customers and their dislikes.

Example: To design the food court in the multiplex the designers analyzed the existing food-courts available in the various malls in different cities for design aspects and to answer the questions "Why it failed in the market?"

Device 30: Research - Need Ring

Need Ring pre-warns the designers about the future changes in the market.

This device is useful in anticipating and designing new services much before they would be demanded in the market.

This concept is based upon the concept of need and demand. Need is the requirements of the market but all is not demanded by the consumers. Demand is the smaller circle inside the need circle. Demand is the immediate requirement of the market. This means that some portion of the need is not yet demanded. If we could create a thin ring above the demand circle, it becomes the 'Need Ring'. This ring consists of the requirements of the market, which are not yet demanded, but would soon be demanded. The marketers and designers need to analyze this ring. The current trends and macro factors of the market would help in analyzing the constituents of the need ring. Designers need to develop services for this ring as these services would soon be demanded in the market.

<u>Example</u>: Steve Jobs was the master in identifying the need rings in the market and developing the quality services which would be embraced by the market.

Device 31: Research - Design Attraction

Understand the design features which pull the people to consume the services in the market.

This analysis would give deeper understanding to the designers about the design features which would be valued by the consumers.

Identify the successful services in the market and check for consumer feedback about the respected design aspects of these services, which attract these consumers. Capture all the valued design elements and ideas of the chosen services. This understanding would be useful for designing the new services for the market.

Example: To design a new 'office reception area' check for all the popular sitting areas in the market and understand their unique design aspects.

Device 32: Research - Customer Financials

Understand the financial strength of the customer segment so as to design service which suits their budget and expenditure.

This device is helpful in designing services which would be consumed in the market.

Identify the target customer segment in the market. Get the data and information about the budgeting, savings and expenditures of the targeted niche. This information is important in designing the services with pricing well within the budget of the customers.

Example: To design the movie watching experience of the viewers at a movie theatre, the designers got the complete understanding of the consumer financials.

Device 33: Research - Other Values

Identify the other values the service adds to the customer e.g. reputation, glamour.

This understanding is useful in knowing the impact of service design in the life of users, which would guide designers to design better services.

Collect secondary data and conduct primary research to analyze the value additions of the service in the life of the people. Primary surveys, with closed ended questions, can be conducted to understand these values. These surveys would also disclose the role of service design in specified value addition.

Example: A chauffeur service adds support and glamour.

Device 34: Research - Perceptions

Note the various perceptions of the different users about the existing services in the market.

This analysis is useful in getting the complete spectrum of the perceptions existing in the market about the services used by consumers.

Identify services to be analyzed in the market. Check for the various types of the customers in the market, including the extreme users. Note the perceptions of these users and the reasons associated with their specific views. Use this insight in designing the services which would cater to the complete range of users.

Example: To design a new private taxi service the market needs to be analyzed for the various perceptions about the existing related services in the market.

Device 35: Research - Other Industries Marketers

Capture the insights of the marketers from other industries.

This device helps the designer by equipping them with the suggestions and ideas of other professionals who brings in fresh perspectives.

Identify the best marketers of other industries and meet them to take their suggestions and views about the market and the design of your services. These people would bring in new ideas and viewpoints which could help the designers in creating a better service.

Example: The design of a department store was improved with the suggestions of marketers of other industries.

Device 36: Research - Profitability Analysis

Check the long term profitability of the service and forecast it for long term.

This analysis establishes the business case for the service. If the service is not profitable then the service needs to be optimized with design changes.

Analyze the cost of operating the service. Forecast the pricing, revenues and profitability of the service. Is the service operation a viable proposition? If not, the required changes need to be made to the service to build a logical case for its development.

Example: The tours and travel packages were modified to adjust them within the cost and price range of the target customer segment.

Device 37: Research - Feasibility Study

Study the feasibility of delivering the designed service.

This study clarifies the feasibility of operations of the service. If the service is not realistic for delivery, then its design has to be changed to make it a feasible business or it should be scrapped.

Conduct the feasibility analysis of the service looking at all operational aspects in the delivery of the service. Any problem related to the feasibility of the service needs to be undertaken and resolved immediately.

Example: New sealed packages were designed to protect the perishable food items.

Device 38: Research - Macro Analysis

Analyze the service and its positioning on the macro platform.

This is a nice way to have the big-picture view of the service.

Create the charts of the sector and industry and position the service on those charts. Similarly analyze the customer segment served with this service.

Example: A new holiday package was analyzed by marketers for its positioning in the present offerings in the industry.

EXPERIENCE SEGMENT

This segment of READ modal consists of devices which emphasize on the importance of experiencing the service, which would be used by the consumers. These devices reveal hidden areas which are difficult to discuss or observe.

Device 39: Experience - In Other's Shoes

Experience the feelings of the user, while consuming or using the service.

The designer needs to understand the problems and limitations of the special conditions of the consumers for designing the service.

The designers can wear ear plugs or heavy clothing to simulate the limitations of the end-users. These experiences are important to understand the conditions of the users so as to design a right service for the consumers.

Example: While designing the chair for heavy and bulky people at a restaurant the designers wore special clothing and put on extra weight to simulate the experience of the user.

Device 40: Experience - Extreme Consumption

Check for extreme consumers and their various ways which can create problems in service delivery.

This analysis helps in understanding the extreme consumption of the service and in identifying the design modifications which could minimize the problems in service delivery.

Identify the extreme users of the service and check for the eccentric ways the service could be consumed by these people. Considering these users as the future consumers of the service and modify the processes and design of the service to make it more flexible and accommodating.

Example: to design the public playground, the designer considered all types of extreme users of the park to make it more usable by people.

Device 41: Experience - Use as Consumer

Consume the service as consumer.

This is useful to understand, observe and experience the service consumption at the right location, revealing unknown problems and contexts.

Consume the designed service at the delivery point as customer and notify the experiences, feelings and observations while consuming the service.

Example: Designers used the designed online shopping portal posing as various types of customers, at different location, to understand their experiences for improving the shopping experience.

Device 42: Experience - Design Touching Senses

Check for the human senses which would be touched with the service delivery.

This understanding would help in refining the service delivery by making it soothing and gratifying for human senses.

Observe and analyze the various ways in which the service delivery would touch the five human senses of the consumers. Understand its effect on the consumer's feelings and emotions. The design of the service must be pleasurable for the consumers to use.

Example: The design of the 'point of sale' counter was tested for its pleasurable effects on the human senses.

Device 43: Experience - Simulate

The designers should simulate the design of service delivery.

These simulations are important for the evaluation of the concept and helps in revealing the hidden issues and problems, which need attention of the designers. These simulations need to be iterated till a fine design is evolved.

Note down all the finalized concepts of the service and simulate each idea. These ideas need to be tested by designers in various ways to reveal the weaknesses of the idea. This process needs to be repeated till the final working and satisfactory design concept is ready.

Example: The script of the call center executive with the customer was simulated to perfect it.

Device 44: Experience - Interaction Design

Use two dimensional images and designs for testing them for human interactions.

This type of testing is fast and economical to check the design of interfaces.

Use pictures or draw the interfaces on paper or screen to be checked by designers and end users. The experience of using the interfaces would reveal the hidden aspects and problems in the interaction design of the interface. This process can be repeated to optimize the design of the interface.

Example: To design the interface of a software application of touch screen tablet device would involve several interfaces designed on paper or charts and consumers use them to check the consumption experience. The interaction design would be refined with each iteration.

Device 45: Experience - Look into the Future

Let the multifunctional team of the company define the future for their company within the forecasted environment.

This forecast is useful in designing the service which would have long term relevance.

Organize a multifunctional meeting to forecast about the future environment, market and industry. Also, discuss about the changes in the company and its services offering due to these forecasts. The service design needs to suit these forecasts. It is important to note that the design needs to be flexible enough to create the required changes in the service if required.

<u>Example</u>: Designing the data services for corporate based upon the forecasts of the company.

Device 46: Experience - Feel it physically

Setup scenarios and play roles for various users, focusing on the instinctive responses prompted by the physical enactment of the role or situation.

This is useful in testing ideas in various contexts and understanding behavior based responses of the consumers.

<u>Example</u>: The interiors of a long route train were designed by actually creating and enacting various scenarios to create maximum comfort for the travelers.

Device 47: Experience - Rough Model

Designers should test the service ideas immediately in the rough format.

Using rough models the team can visualize the service to be designed.

During the initial process of designing the service test the various service ideas to check for delivery and operations. These models give a physical feel to the service and its macro technicalities can be analyzed. These basic models graduate to the working models of the service.

Example: While designing a coffee shop, several rough models were created before developing the working model of the service.

Device 48: Experience - Various Users Testing

Check the design of the service with various set of customer segments.

Different customers consume the service in various ways which can illuminate the designers about any hidden problems with the design of the service.

Identify the various potential customer segments of the service and ask them to experience the service in various ways. Check for the deficiencies in the service.

Example: Check the interaction of the reception staff at the emergency section of the hospital with various segments from the population.

Device 49: Experience - Consumption Stories

Create visual stories of consuming the service in various ways and let the potential customers comment on it for gaps.

This device helps in understanding the potential value of the service and helps in improving the characteristics of the service.

Create videos and pictures of the various events when the service would be delivered and ask future users to share their views.

Example: Create video stories of people using a new design of hotel lobby in various ways and situations and users were asked to comment on these stories.

Device 50: Experience - Use it

Let designers consume the designed service with non-project people like their friends, colleagues and family members.

Using the services designed by them the designers have the experience of the end users of the service and they will be able to innovate better.

Ask the designers to consume the service, designed and executed by them, for certain amount of time to find problems with the design.

Example: Designers used the first prototype of the designed retail store for one week to check for the expected value addition and look to scope of improvement in experience.

Device 51: Experience - Limitations

Check for the limitations for using the service.

This is important to clarify the expectations of the consumers from the service.

The service should be tested with minimum and maximum parameters to check for its limitations.

Example: Check for the limitations of the public utility services.

Device 52: Experience - Live With Them

Designers live with the various consumers like their family members to understand them better.

This method is extremely useful to understand the attitudes, behaviors, emotions and feeling of the consumers.

Choose consumers from various categories of the customer segments and stay with them as their family members while regularly taking text, audio, video and picture notes to understand their thinking, psychology and decisions. Analyze these notes to design a suitable service for them.

Example: To design a family holiday package the designers stayed with the potential customer's families to understand their unspecified requirements.

Device 53: Experience - Precautions

Check for the precautions for consuming the service.

This analysis is extremely important to keep the safety of the users into consideration.

Identify all the ways in which the service delivery can affect the user negatively. The design of the service should take into consideration all these aspects. Precautions to use the service should be specified clearly and communicated to the potential consumers in best possible ways.

Example: To use any adventure sport the precautions should be clearly communicated to the consumers in such a way that even a layman can understand it clearly.

Device 54: Experience - Existing Users

Analyze the existing users consuming the similar services.

This process acquaints the designers with various ways the service would be used.

Identify a set of similar services available in the market. Analyze the regular users of these services and note the various ways the service is being delivered and consumed by them.

Example: To design a new office environment designers interacted with various employees of several offices to take their feedback about their office environment.

Device 55: Experience - Service Integration

Check for various ways the service gets integrated in consumer's life.

Let users record with pictures, videos and written facts about the various ways the service gets embedded in the user's life.

Give users cameras and ask them to record the use of the service by capturing pictures and videos.

Example: The online music stores were analyzed for their role in the life of the consumers who regularly use it to enjoy music and songs.

Device 56: Experience - Designer Perception

Check for the perception of designers about the customer experiences.

This is useful to contrast the perceived and actual experiences and feelings of the customers.

Record the actual experiences of the customers while consuming the services. Use pictures, audios, videos and descriptions to record these consumer's experiences. Ask the designers to describe in detail the experiences and emotional states of the customers while using the services. Present the gap in the understanding of the designers.

Example: Designers were asked to explain their understanding about the experiences of the people at a hospital. Gaps in their understanding were presented to them by showing them the videos of actual consumption of the service with the experiences described by the consumers.

ANALYZE SEGMENT

This segment of READ model focuses on different ways the consumers are analyzed through observations and recordings. The devices in Analyze segment aims to understand the problem areas and innovation opportunities through studying their actions and behaviors.

Device 57: Analyze - Invisible Presence

Record and analyze the actions and behaviors of the consumers while performing the activity without disturbing them in any way.

This analysis helps in getting the clarity about the actual activities performed by the users in real time, which is much better than asking them about describing their actions.

Identify the activities related to the service and observe people performing them. The presence of the designers needs to be invisible which means that they observe the actions performed by the people without interfering them in any way.

Example: Designers observed and analyzed the sales professionals giving sales presentations to understand the need for a suitable and impactful ways for presentation.

Device 58: Analyze - Other Service's Consumption

Check for the ways the other services are consumed by people.

This analysis helps in giving information about the various ways the service would be consumed.

Identify the services to be analyzed for consumption. Observe and record the people consuming those services. This analysis specifies the various factors which can improve the service design.

Example: To design a breaking news service the consumers were analyzed for their consumption of existing news and information services through various media.

Device 59: Analyze – Customer Behavior in Stores

Record and analyze the consumer behavior of the customers to understand their thinking process during the consumption of services.

This analysis helps in clarifying the other design parameters which attracts and motivates the consumers to consume the service.

Use video cameras at strategic locations at department stores and shops to observe people while they make the consumer decisions. Analyze this data to understand the decision making process of consumers to consume the services.

Example: Installation of video cameras in a toy store clarified the designers about the visual parameters which impacts the customer decisions of the customers.

Device 60: Analyze - New Service and Life

Check the various ways in which the designed service gets integrated with the life of the consumers.

This information is useful by clarifying the potential and future uses of the service.

Discuss with the potential customers about the various way the service would be consumed and its importance in their life.

Example: Analyze the various ways in which a new directory service gets integrated into the life of the consumer and its value addition in people's life.

Device 61: Analyze – Weak Points

Check for various ways when the service would not be delivered properly during its consumption.

This understanding would compel the designers to improve the design of the service to make it more flexible.

Ask the participants to consume the service naturally and observe the various events when the service could not be delivered properly. These events should be analyzed to improve the service design.

Example: To design a live data service, it was used by various people to check for any gaps which could affect the service delivery.

Device 62: Analyze - Innovative Consumption of Service

Check for various ways the service would be used by consumers.

This analysis is helpful in creating the design of the service which would satisfy various users.

Check the design of the service with various categories of users and observe them over a period of time for different ways the service is used by consumers.

Example: A new location based social network application was used to connect better with friends and receive real-time effective feedbacks.

Device 63: Analyze - Capture Pictures

Capture the pictures of objects and people doing certain activities related to the design project.

This device helps in identifying the patterns of behaviors of consumers during certain activities.

Capture the photographs of people during specific time performing certain activities to understand their habits and behavioral patterns.

Example: Designers captured pictures of people cooking food to understand various patterns for designing the service to improve their efficiency.

Device 64: Analyze - Project Visits

Escort the consumers on the service design related visits and observe their experiences and thinking.

This is useful in notifying the feelings and experiences of the participants in real time. This exercise would produce the effective information and insights which cannot be generated during simple interview.

Take consumer's permission to accompany them on relevant visits, which are related to service design. Observe, notify and capture the real-time ideas, observations and thinking of the participants.

Example: Designers accompanied the shoppers in the department store to look for ways to improve their shopping experience.

Device 65: Analyze - Daily Objects

Identify the objects which the potential consumers interacts with every day.

This observation generates insights about the objects which customers use during consumption of service. This understanding would help the designer to design services which can integrate easily with the life of the customers.

Interact with the customers of the service to understand the objects they use and interact with every day. Also, check the various ways these things are used and carried, and the effect they could have on the designed service.

Example: to design the economy hotel room the designers analyzed the target customers for the objects they use and carry during travelling.

Device 66: Analyze - Become their Friend

Visit and spend time with the users during the specific consumption time of the service.

This exercise helps the designer to observe the people consuming the service in real time, over a period of time.

Check for the specific time of the day when the service is used and visit them for several days to observe its consumption by them.

Example: Designers checked people for the usage of the social networking service using their laptop or PC, using Wi-Fi.

Device 67: Analyze - Service and Life

Check the various ways in which the existing service gets integrated with the life of the consumers.

This information is useful by clarifying the future uses of the service.

Follow the consumers for few days and collect information about the service consumption at various intervals. Analyze the value propositions of the service in the life of customers. Prepare detailed uses of the service.

Example: Analyze the various ways in which a smartphone gets integrated into the life of the consumer and its value delivery through various applications.

Device 68: Analyze - Body Double

Accompany potential users to understand their routine and interactions.

This is a powerful way to reveal design opportunities and show how a service might affect or complement user's behaviors and actions.

Move with potential users to observe and understand their day-to-day routines, interactions and contexts.

Example: Designers accompanied the school kids to design a better school experience for them.

Device 69: Analyze - Social Connections

Identify the various relationships, connections and flow of information between a group and network.

This is useful in understanding the official, casual and interpersonal relationships between networks and smaller groups and the flow of information between them.

Create 2D or 3D diagrams and models to capture the social connections between the groups and networks.

Example: Social connection analysis helped a big organization to improve the communication between its various departments and regions.

Device 70: Analyze – Service Complaints

Find the various ways the service can create the problems for consumers.

This analysis is important to understand the service elements which need to be avoided.

Designers should test the service delivery extensively in various conditions, places and circumstances for possible problems which can be caused with the consumption of the service.

<u>Example</u>:

The new information delivery service was tested extensively, in all possible conditions, for their accuracy and promptness.

Device 71: Analyze - Supporting Service

Check for the supporting service or product required to deliver the designed service.

This analysis would be helpful in creating a solution for the market.

Analyze the various ways the designed service would be used by different categories of customers. Check for the supporting service or product which would be required to use it.

Example: A luxury car service was required by new hotel to serve its customers better.

Device 72: Analyze - How They Live?

Observe the consumers when they live in the house.

This observation would reveal hidden opportunities for innovation.

Put video cameras in the people's home at relevant place and record their daily activities. This observation may open up the possibilities of developing services which could make their life better and productive.

Example: An opportunity for preparing meals faster was found by observing their time spend in kitchen.

Device 73: Analyze - All Categories of Customers

Analyze the service design and its delivery for its suitability for all categories of customers.

The analysis is important in expanding the size of the market.

Divide the target customer segment into various categories. Analyze and test the service design suiting the requirements of all categories.

Example: A business software should function in various languages to serve the various customers segments of different countries.

Device 74: Analyze - Consumer's Habits

Understand and record the habits of the consumers.

This is helpful in creating services which would get better integrated into their lives.

Observe the potential consumers performing tasks in context of the service design and observe the habits and behaviors. The designers should consider these facts in the service design which would better integrate in people's life.

Example: The seating behavior of the people was observed and analyzed by designers to design the seating arrangement for a public park.

Device 75: Analyze - Video Capture

Use video cameras to record movements of people and objects in a space over a prolonged period of time.

This is useful in providing a macro view of the space within the context of the project.

Finalize the space to be analyzed for a design project and put video cameras (infra-red enabled) to record every movement in the space over a large period of time. These videos can be speed viewed to understand the usage of space.

Example: The reception area of a big company was observed for several weeks to redesign it for better usage.

Device 76: Analyze - Consumer Day

Spend a day with consumer to understand their experiences and feelings.

This is important to check for unexpected issues and problems which the consumers experience every day.

Accompany a consumer for the whole day, without interfering them in any way, and notify your observations of their experiences and problems they face. This exercise can provide opportunities for innovation.

Example: A cosmetic company conducted analysis of ladies traveling during summers to develop a skin care service.

Device 77: Analyze - Personal Productivity

Observe people at work and check for their various habits which make them more productive.

This exercise would act like an idea bank as each observation would give designers a new idea for personal productivity.

Observe the large number of people during their work time and notify minutely the specific actions which make them productive and efficient. This exercise is especially effective while observing them meeting their deadlines or completing the urgent work.

Exercise: The observation of the 100 sales managers over a period of three months gave wealth of insights about the new ways to store important information using pen and paper.

Device 78: Analyze - Movement Patterns

Observe and notify the usage of a space by people over a period of time.

These observations help the designers to analyze the usage of a space and specific behavioral patterns.

Divide the space to be analyzed into several equal segments and observe its usage over a period of time to notify its usage by people. Designers can identify several patterns of the people while using the space.

Example: Designers observed a train platform for its consumption to analyze the movement patterns of the commuters.

DISCOVER SEGMENT

Discover segment of READ model includes devices which focuses on the various ways the designers interact directly with the consumers to understand their views, requirements, desires and perceptions.

Device 79: Discover - Segmented Users Testing

Segment the users and test each of them, in detail, to get their views about the service.

This analysis would give designers various ideas and hidden problems related to the service characteristics and delivery.

Segment the users of the service and test its design with all types of categories of people. Let them openly comment, give suggestions and share experiences about the service. This process needs to be repeated till each segment looks satisfied with the service.

Example: The interaction design of a web portal for travelling services was tested with various segments of users to refine its design for user friendliness.

Device 80: Discover - Customer's Dislikes

Understand the dislikes of the customer in the existing services, so that designers could be careful in future designs.

This understanding cautions the designers about the aspects and characteristics they need to avoid in the design.

Identify the similar services existing in the market and survey the consumers for each service for the characteristics of the service and its delivery which are detested by them. Also, check for the reasons for the specified dislikes. This information can be used to design better services which would be liked by the market, even by the fierce critics.

Example: To design an entertainment television channel, the market was scanned for the areas which are disliked by the consumers in existing channels on television.

Device 81: Discover - Ask for Features

Ask the potential consumers about the features which they would like to have in the service.

This analysis creates a list of features which are desired by the consumers.

Conduct an extensive survey covering all the categories of the customers to understand their requirements and expectations from the service. All these features can be listed to create a final feature list for the service design.

Example: To design a new readymade garment store the market was surveyed for the features which the consumers would 'love to have' and 'must have'.

Device 82: Discover - Feature Priorities

Ask the potential consumers about the priority of features they would like to have in the service.

This analysis helps in finalizing the list of features which would be included in the final service.

Compile the list of service features which would be desired by the market. Conduct an extensive survey covering all the categories of the customers to understand their requirements and priority of the specified features. The final list of features can be made from priority listing of features.

Example: To design a new readymade garment store the market was surveyed for the priority of features in the service.

Device 83: Discover - Customer Journal

Ask the consumers to create a journal of their day with pictures, audio, videos and descriptions.

This journal would help the designers to understand their customers better.

Create a 'Daily Journal Kit' for the consumers, which would help them to record their day with text, photos, audios and videos. Ask the participants to record their day with descriptions. This recording needs to be general and not specific to any specific task or act. These journals can be analyzed for deepening their understanding the customer segment, which would help designers to create emphatic services.

Example: A design company keeps collecting the customer journals to use them as their competitive advantage in designing and deliver successful services.

Device 84: Discover - Customer Feedback

Check the customer feedback for the existing services.

This survey is helpful in understanding the views of the customers about the services in the market, which could help the designers to integrate the positive feedback and learn from the negative feedback to improve their service designs. These surveys can be macro or on any specific micro level.

Identify the popular but similar services in the market and conduct the extensive feedback analysis. This analysis can also be available in the market as a secondary research. Understand the perceptions, experiences and feelings about these services.

Example: Before designing a new news portal the designers conducted the extensive feedback research for news services present in the market and other sources of breaking news.

Device 85: Discover - Service Value

How do consumers value the service in their life?

This analysis is helpful in knowing the value proposition of the service and features responsible for delivering this value.

Interact with a set of consumers to understand the value addition by the service in their lives. Check for the features and elements responsible for this value addition. Design the processes to enhance the value proposition of the service.

Example: The value proposition of the mobile application of a weather channel was analyzed to understand its utility value. New features were added to this application to enhance its value.

Device 86: Discover - Cross Question

Question the consumers repeatedly to understand the fundamental reasons for using a service.

This information is helpful in understanding their behaviors, decisions and attitudes in context of a service.

Prepare a large list of questions and cross questions to make the consumer reveal the underlying reason for their decisions and actions. The set of cross questions would help the designers to dig deeper into their psyche and understand them better.

Example: Designers used cross questions to understand the actual reasons of consumers to use a specific brand of hair care service.

Device 87: Discover - Conceptualize

Use images to develop and explain a concept

This exercise is used to understand the ideas and perceptions of issues and helps consumers to specify complex or unexplainable themes.

To understands the consumer's perception about the evolution of new technology the participants were asked to conceptualize their perception by using pictures and other visuals.

Device 88: Discover - Other Markets

Understand and analyze the services used in other markets including international markets.

This information would help the designers to understand international design principles and standards.

Identify the international markets and the services to be analyzed and conduct a cross-cultural study to understand the general and specific international design principles. This would help the designers to study the consumption of the services in the various environments and contexts in which the services are used.

Example: Analysis of distance education services gave the designers the new insights about the new education service to be designed.

Device 89: Discover - Think Aloud

Ask the consumers to speak their thinking while performing some specific activities.

This is an effective way to understand their ideas, thinking, perceptions, motivations and reasons.

Identify the tasks in the context of the design project and meet consumers while performing those tasks. Ask them to speak out all of their thinking while performing the task. The designers need to record these and analyze these points to understand them in relation to the service design.

Example: Asking people to think aloud while preparing breakfast gave designers the idea about developing nutritious food with minimal amount of time to prepare.

Device 90: Discover - Interviewing

Interview consumers to understand their ideas and perceptions.

This exercise helps in getting the views from a large number of people about a specific area in least amount of time.

Prepare a set of open-ended and closed-ended questions to survey a sample of target segment. The answers can be collected in controlled situations. These answers reveal certain ideas, perceptions and views about the consumers.

Example: Interviewing helped designers to understand the modifications required in the recently launched educational service in the market.

Device 91: Discover - Focus Groups

Ask various categories of potential customers to discuss and share ideas about the service.

This discussion raises various points and generates ideas and expectations of customers about the new service, features and its design.

For a certain service idea categorize the target customers into various segments. Conduct the discussions and meetings with these potential customers. These meetings can be conducted into various formats ranging from category-wise to mixed teams. These ideas and views can be recorded, which can be analyzed to finalize the design parameters of the service.

Example: To design a new phone based directory service, several dedicated and mixed meetings were conducted with the potential customers to get ideas to enhance its value proposition.

Device 92: Discover - Word Design

Check how consumers associate words with specific design concepts and features.

This exercise helps to prioritize the design concepts and features of the service to be designed.

Ask participants to associate expressive words with diverse design concepts or features in order to show how they perceive and value the issues.

Example: To design a new training program of sales participants were asked to choose and prioritize the various aspects of the program.

Device 93: Discover - Requirement Analysis

Document and analyze the requirements of the consumers.

This analysis clarifies the demand of the market.

Discuss the proposed service with the potential consumers and understand their demands and desires. Analyze them to finalize the feature-set of the service to be designed.

Example: To design a new mobile based organizer and planner the market was scanned for the new requirements of the customers and the price they are ready to pay for the enhanced service.

Device 94: Discover - Meet Critics

Meet the biggest service design critics and understand their views.

This analysis would bring in fresh professional views, which can be integrated with other insights to design the service.

Identify the major service critics in the market and meet them for their views about a great service. Check for your learning from the discussions and use these insights to improve the service design.

Example: The views and suggestions of the movie critics were used to create a next successful film by a Hollywood movie director.

Device 95: Discover - Other Markets

Get the views and experiences of the customers from other markets.

This analysis gives new perspective to the design of the service of the consumers from other cultures and demographics.

Identify the relevant markets for analysis and conduct a survey to understand their views about the service design and features.

Example: To design a new managerial cabin in office, consumers from other markets were also consulted for their views on the good design to create a better environment inside the cabin.

Device 96: Discover - Buyer Thinking Process

Understand the thinking process of the customers.

This analysis is helpful in clarifying the aspects of the service which make the customer to decide on buying the service.

The experts in the consumer psychology can help in understanding the thinking process of the consumers. This understanding would help the designers to integrate the required features and aspects which would support in increasing the sale of the service.

Example: To design a better packaging of washing powder the consumers were observed and analyzed at various retail stores.

Device 97: Discover - Perceptions

Check for various perceptions about the service.

This analysis is important to understand perception of the service to predict the future consumption of the service.

Meet people from various customer segments to understand the various perceptions they have about the service and the various ways it could add value.

<u>Example</u>: Look for the various perceptions about an online marketplace of mobile applications.

Device 98: Discover - Picture Book

Motivate the participants to record their views and experiences on a notebook, in expressive format.

This device exposes the hidden point of views and expectations of the customers.

Ask participants to prepare a picture book, which includes pictures and descriptions, about their impressions, circumstances, and activities related to the service.

Example: Participants were asked to record their experiences with new digital camera on a pleasure trip to a beach.

Device 99: Discover - Card Organization

Ask participants to organize cards in the most logical and suitable order, to understand their mental models about a service.

This exercise helps to expose people's mental models about a system. Their arrangement reveals expectations and priorities about the intended features and functions.

On separate cards, name possible features, characteristics or design attributes. Ask people to organize the cards logically, in ways that make sense to them.

Example: Participants were asked to organize a vacant living room in the best possible way, to understand their priorities about luxury items in their home.

Device 100: Discover - Navigation Charts

Understand the navigation used by the participants.

This is a useful way to discover the significant elements, pathways, and other spatial behavior associated with a real or virtual environment.

Ask participants to map an existing or virtual space and understand their navigation process.

Example: The plan & schedule of courier deliveries was analyzed to understand the navigation used by them to improve efficiency.

Device 101: Discover - Cultural Differences

Ask people of different cultures to note their feelings and experiences about a specific task.

This analysis is important to understand the views, perceptions and behaviors within or across cultures.

Identify the cultures to conduct the analysis. Prepare a template diary and ask them to note their views, feelings and experiences while doing the specified activity. This information can be analyzed to understand the differences between them.

Example: To design a better dining experience the designers asked the participants to notify their views and experiences while using the dining table of their home.

Device 102: Discover - Visualize and Draw

Ask participants to visualize an experience and draw it on paper.

This exercise reveals the unspecified but important aspects of an experience. This also reveals their feelings and perception about the event.

Ask the participants to think about an experience, which would be in context of the service design and draw it on paper. The analysis of these drawing would reveal the genuine experiences and expectations of the consumers.

Example: The experiences of consumers at a bank branch were understood with the specified method to create a better environment at the branch.

About Author

Anshuman is an entrepreneur and investor and has been instrumental in nurturing many successful companies. He has created of several successful companies in various domains. He is also involved in supporting development of several other companies. In business, his interests lie in cutting edge technologies and innovative services.

His guidance has helped many businessman, investors and entrepreneurs to succeed in their businesses. He has also supported several entrepreneurship cells and incubation centers.

He is an engineer and a management graduate. He can be reached at anshuman.connect@gmail.com